THE MANUAL,
REAL ESTATE SUCCESS

Randall Guyton

The Manual, Credit Real Estate Success

ISBN-13: 978-1505263152
ISBN-10: 1505263158

Create Space Independent Publishing Platform

Disclaimer

Table of Contents

Acknowledgment

First I would like to thank God. Without him none of this would be possible. I would have never been able to share with you guys this information. So with that said I give all praises to the Most High!

I would like to thank my beautiful mother, Tanya, and my father, Darnell for everything they have done for me throughout my life. I truly appreciate you both for always supporting and encouraging me to be great!

I would like to also thank my biggest supporter, the beautiful Racquel, for always supporting me and being my backbone through everything. You are the reason I wrote this book. You always said that God gave me a gift to share and you believed in me at times when I didn't believe in myself. Thank you my queen.

I would like to thank my brother from another mother, Arthur R. You've always been a major support system my entire life. We experienced some of the greatest and lowest times together and I truly thank God for allowing me to experience them with you.

Finally, I would like to thank the rest of my family and friends who have always supported me and encouraged me to be great. I'm sorry I couldn't mention you all by name, but I want you to know that you are extremely appreciated. Your efforts have not gone unnoticed.

I love you all!

Introduction

Before we begin, allow me the chance to clear the air. This is not a get rich quick scheme. If you're looking for a book that's going to give you some type of false hope with fake strategies that never work then this is not it. If you're looking for a read from an author who was bred from day one to be a top selling, published author then this is not the book for you either.

But if you are looking for guidance from someone who knows how it feels to not know or to struggle and watch family members do the same, but somehow made it out and is now willing to share with you his strategies so that you can do the same, then I must say my friend you are in the right place.

Let's get to the proper introduction. My name is Randall Guyton, and I am the President of South East Financial, which is one of the most successful Credit Restoration Companies based out of South Florida. I was born and raised in Miami Florida, but not the Miami Florida you may be familiar with. Not The South Beach, high rise, condo, fast cars and pretty woman Miami Florida that tends to be promoted through all marketing materials to attract tourism. No, I grew up across the bridge in one of the most dangerous areas in the United States, a part of town you will never see on any marketing material. It is a small area by the name of Liberty City.

I'm sure you have an idea by now that things weren't so well and great. I was not born with a silver spoon in my mouth, or college tuition paid for. I was raised by two very hard working parents who both did not receive a college degree. They worked their hearts out to give me and my siblings the best life that they could. So with that said Thank you Mom and Dad.

Despite my parents not being the richest, or college educated they still provided me with a vast amount information that I could use mentally in life, which in reality allowed me to use those same teachings to help me succeed financially.

Growing up, and spending 18 years in Liberty city was not easy. We lived from paycheck to paycheck in a 2 bedroom apartment with me and my oldest brother in one room, and my Oldest sister in another. My mother slept on the sofa in our living room to allow my eldest sister the opportunity to have her own room because she was the only girl. Now I know what you're getting at. Where was Dad? Unfortunately my mother and father divorced right after I was born. My dad moved on with his life and my mother moved on with hers.

Regardless of their divorce, they both continued to maintain a good relationship with one another to help co-parent and raise us to the best of their ability. Outside of God and my family, I give all thanks to where I came from.

Growing up in Liberty City exposed me to a lot. One of the most valuable lessons I was taught everyday growing up was seeing people daily I did not want to become. Failure and the results from wrong decisions were very much alive in my eyes. Everyone around me struggled. Many of my neighbors lacked higher education, and most people I grew up with could never see themselves doing anything greater than what they were already doing. If it was not for God, my mother and father installing what they actually installed in me, I would probably be a product of my environment and you would not be reading this book today. So again I give thanks to all.

Yes, I say thanks a lot. I'm a firm believer in appreciating all that is given to me, and never becoming so big that I forget who help me get where I am today. So that's a lesson within itself. Always remember to give thanks.

The reason why I took time to write this book was because I wanted to provide something that can change lives. With all my experience through the good and the bad, I learned a great deal of information about credit, understanding credit, repairing credit, and using real estate and real estate investing to get me where I actually wanted to be in life, which was controlling my finances. I understood those things so well that eventually, at a very young age of 23, I started executing theses same strategies that I'm about to share with you today. I must say things begun to go really well for me by doing so, but it got to a point where I started to look back at myself and say, "Hey, things are going well for me but what about my siblings, friends, and people I may have known from my upbringing." Everyone appeared to be stuck in the same place.

Eventually I moved my mother from that small apartment in Liberty City, and I moved away as well. I would never see anyone from my old neighborhood in my new location, not even the ones who were just like me. I never saw them in my new environment, and it felt like everyone just disappeared. I decided to start taking short trips back to my old neighborhood. I felt I grew unattached and I was very curious what was actually taking place now. I was in total shock with what I saw. Everyone seemed to be in a bad space. I'm sure it's because I was no longer there and moved on but the conditions seemed worse than before.

After a few short visits, I decided to find a way to help. I knew what life had to offer and all the information that was available. If I didn't attempt to try, to show, to teach, to allow others, just like me, an opportunity to create a better future for their lives, and their family, I wouldn't have been able to live with myself because of that selfish act.

Now with that said I hope by now you have a clear understanding of why this book was written. The purpose is to give you the opportunity to do the same things that I did, so get very familiar with this book. Everything about it, from start to finish, will be your life line. This book has all the secrets you need to attack life at full force and succeed. I need you to view this book with a great deal of importance, like a manual, a financial life guidance bible. By following these steps and pounding all this information in your head consistently will help you get where you need to be, financially in control. The choice is up to you. I can only tell you the things I did, the strategies that may have worked for me or may have not worked, or what's working for me now. I can give you all the information I know, but at the end of the day the only person who has the right to change your life is you. You must say to yourself "I want better. I want more. I deserve more." Then take the necessary actions to make this a reality.

I conduct regular seminars and daily coaching's and I can tell you the biggest mistakes I have seen people make is to just talk, but never take action. We all know everyone loves good news, everyone loves the hope speech, and the "Maybe I can be better" or "Do better" speech. But no one takes action. Fact is, you can read this book a thousand times; you can carry this book with you everywhere, but if you do not take action to incorporate the techniques you will learn in this book into your daily life, I can promise you one thing; come next year this time you will be in the same place you were this year at the start of this book.

Now that you guys know who I am, where I come from, and what I'm here to do, let's get right into it.

Ground Zero - Understanding Credit

I know the title states Credit Real Estate Success, and I'm sure that's what you are here to achieve, but before you can even think of real estate, or picture yourself owning a property for personal or rental, your fist step must be to understand credit. If you don't understand anything else you must understand this.

It is import to have great credit and there are benefits that come from it. Credit is everything. It can open doors like you never imagined. Credit can get you that nice home you want, that vehicle you always felt you deserved, credit cards you may need to leverage your monthly cash flow, or whatever else you may feel you need, credit can provide. By understanding the value of credit and how extremely important it is you can make your life and achieving financial control a whole lot easier.

I think the biggest mistake we make coming from what I like to call the no silver spoon background is the lack of knowledge about credit and how important it really is. We tend to get caught in the phrase that cash wins everything. We sometimes get to a point where we believe that if we put ourselves in a position to be stable with cash then we don't need credit. I can just pay things off and I would never owe anyone. I tried that, and it was a big mistake. Not only did I deplete my savings, I was not in the best financial situation to afford homes and cars. The little cash I had left could only be used to rent and purchase used cars from dealers that did not require credit checks. Those very bad decisions restricted me from never owning my own home and my cars were never new.

It's pretty sad because a lot of people right now are living in what we call at South East Financial "Credit Prison". They are never able to purchase a home, or a new car, and they are always paying high interest rates for everything. The knowledge to escape eludes them. But guess what? Everything you need to know is right here. By understanding credit and how it works, your life can become a whole lot easier, regardless of your current financial situation.

Understanding what credit really is and what a credit report is can truly save you a lot of time and headache. So Let's get to it!

What's A Credit Report?

A credit report is the result of a query that has been run on a group of databases owned and operated by the credit bureaus. When a credit report is pulled a query is ran on all the bureaus databases in order to compile information that is hopefully related to a specific consumer. The problem with this is that this system tends to not always work at its best as some bureaus tend to use last name and first initials in order to match data with the consumer. Maybe it's just me, but talk about being set up to lose from the beginning. I'm sure you can see where the problem lies with this method.

There can be many consumers in your state with your same last name and first name initials, so the chances of you receiving data that is not yours is extremely high. This results in you suffering for someone else's mistakes without even knowing it. I have seen time and time again new credit profiles on a daily basis with data being reported that's not even accurate. A recent study by the National Association of State Public Interest Research Groups discovered that 79 percent of all credit reports contain some type of errors. I hope by now you can get an understanding of why contacting a credit repair expert is very important. You can potentially have data on your report that's not even yours which in reality will keep you from taking control of your finances.

Now that you are more familiar with what credit is and how it is reported the next best step would be to have your current credit report pulled. This by far is one of the most important steps pertaining to credit. You can't even think about repairing or fixing your credit if you have not done this. Without this you are lost and the game will not start.

Getting your credit report once a year and getting an update on what's being reported is one of the best decisions you can make, and doing this is quite simply. There are plenty of websites that you can go to which would allow you to pull it for free. For example, annualcreditreport.com allows you to pull your credit report once a year free of charge.

Now after receiving your current report, get familiar with all that's being reported and make note of anything you believe is not accurate. Once that's completed your next step would be to contact your local credit repair expert, or you can begin to dispute all inaccurate debts yourself if you feel up to it. There are plenty of sites that can assist you with free dispute letters, but consider the fact that millions of others will be using those same letters, so the chances are very low that you would see any positive results from this. Also, before you begin to dispute, keep in mind that not all debt are considered bad debt, and some debt removal can actually hurt your credit score so I advise you to have a very clear understanding of the disputing process before taking matters in your own hands. But the choice remains yours.

I support anyone who believes they have what it takes to take on the dispute process themselves, but I'm also a firm believer in allowing the experts to do what they do best. It's about working smarter, not harder.

Now I know you have tried a so called credit repair expert who did not get the job done and did not deliver on any of the promises they may have made. I'm also very aware of the bad eye that is placed over the credit repair business and its companies. I understand completely.

Before I started South East Financial, I dealt with the same thing. I went off to college and made multiple mistakes as it relates to my finances. Because of my then current financial situation, I was desperate. I started applying for cards and student loans just to get by, and when it was time to clean up all those bad decisions I made early on I had a hard time finding someone I could trust in the credit repair industry to assist. That was one of the reasons I started taking the credit repair business so serious and taking the steps to learn and understand it the way that I do today. I have been jerked on many occasions before I decided that enough was enough. I understand if you are a little skeptical when it comes to hiring a credit repair expert, but my advice to you is to remember that this is an investment in your future. Don't just do a Google search and hire the first person you see. Do your homework. Contact multiple credit repair companies in your city and state. Find out their certifications and what qualifies them for it; find out there price points and the programs they offer; and really just get a full understanding of them and how you could actually benefit from using their services. The person you hire will potentially change your life for the better or worse, so make sure to make your decision based on that train of thought. This is not a joke. This is your life we are talking about and I don't know about you, but I don't play when it comes to my life.

Here is when it starts to get good. Once you have decided what company works best for you and make the decision to start their program, it's time to start seeing results. But remember patience is everything. There's no secret clean credit in 10 days remedy, and if someone is offering that I advise you to run the opposite direction because chances are they are doing something illegal.

I always advise all my clients to allow us at least three to six months to start seeing amazing results. But don't be surprised if positive results come even sooner. Now another very important key to building great credit comes from what you do. One thing that I teach and advise all my current clients is to understand the value of positive credit being reported. We must help each other. I can delete all the negative debt off your account but if you have no positive credit being reported, your credit strength and score will only go up so much. You must build positive credit. 35% of your FICO score is determined by your payment history. This means the more new accounts you have reported on your credit report monthly, increases your score if bills are paid on time. How do you get new accounts if your credit is not so great? There are plenty of ways to do this, but I will share with you some of the more effective and easy ones you can get started with today.

Applying For Secured Credit Cards

A secured credit card is nothing more than an alternative for individuals who can't get approved for regular unsecured credit cards. It requires you to make a deposit against the cards credit limit. Now the benefit of this is that you can get approved, even with challenging credit. You will start building positive credit, because most cards report to the three major credit bureaus, unlike a prepaid credit card which only allows you to spend and use like a credit card. Get at least 3 secured credit cards, and always keep spending limits lower than 30% to really start seeing great results. The more you can get the better, but if you only get one, then that's still a good start, but always remember to eventually work towards another.

Go To Your Local Bank And Get A Secure Loan

I know you're like huh, but it's really simple. Here's what you do: Go to your local bank and open up a CD account, and then have a loan secured against that account. Take at least three months before paying off the entire loan. That way it gets reported in your favor with the credit bureaus. This will get you on the road to building that positive credit as quickly as possible, while you hire a credit expert to delete the negative and unfavorable items off your report.

Once you have established those things, just continue to repeat as much as you possibly can, while your credit repair expert work on your debts and dispute process. Within 3 to 6 months you should see an amazing change for the better in your credit report. Doors will be open for you like never before. It may seem like 6 months is too long, but always remember this cannot be done overnight. My grandmother always said, "It's easy to get into debt, but hard to get out" so remember that!

While on the road to credit freedom you must remember to change your mental disposition as well. You must start viewing good credit as a way of life, stay alert as it relates to your current credit situation and what's being reported, and always work to improve it. If you follow my advice, you will never find yourself in the place that you are in today.

This information may not instantly change your situation today, but it can change it for life, and by following you will never find yourself in "Credit Prison" again.

The Value Of Credit And Real Estate

How can credit and real estate change your life financially? I know you're ready to make some money, so here it is.

Firstly, let's clear the air. When I spoke on changing your life financially I was never speaking on just making money, but also on how you can start saving. One thing I'm sure you know is that owning is a lot more beneficial than renting, and in case you don't know here are three reasons why:

Number 1 - Renting a home cost a lot less initially than owning one and this is because the property you are renting is only yours temporally. Just think about it. You will be dishing out money on a monthly basis, but will never receive anything back from it. All you have gained is a roof over your head. But when you decide to own the money that you will be spending every month to maintain a mortgage is working for you by allowing your property to build equity, which you can pull out at a later time to do just about anything you want to do with that free cash. I'm not advising you to just go crazy and spend it all, but the fact that you have those options is a big plus.

Number 2 - Owning a home is a lot less stressful. Anything can happen while renting. Your landlord can stop paying the mortgage, the taxes, or even providing maintenance to upkeep the property which can lead to an unhealthy stay, and a potential sudden move out. I'm sure you can never get a good night's sleep knowing that your living situation is ultimately in another person's hands. I couldn't. Renting also involves more fees to keep track of, such as initial cost and security deposits that do not come with owning a home.

Number 3 - Owning a home can be a very valuable asset in today's unstable economy. It gives you the assurance of knowing that you will always have a place to live. Also one of my favorites when it comes to owning a home is the flexibility to lease your property, or sell it for any reason, which results in a profit gained in most circumstances. Now that's something you could never have the option to do while renting. With that being said I'm sure you now have a clear understanding of why Real estate and credit works hand and hand.

Just look at it this way. Without credit you can never own real estate unless you're in a position to pay for the property with cash, or you found an amazing deal that the seller agreed to hold the mortgage (basically they will play the bank and you pay a monthly fee to them) which does not happen very often. Let's face it, if you are reading this book right now, those chances are slim to none.

Minister Louis Farrakhan wrote, *"As long as we don't have land then somebody else will be the producer and we will be the consumer, so start buying land."*[1]

1

http://www.finalcall.com/artman/publish/Minister_Louis_Farrakhan_9/
article_8360.shtml

Let's Make Some Money With That Credit

So here's the million dollar question, "How can credit allow us to become financially in control by using real estate?"

There are plenty ways I can answer this question but I'm going to give you the simplest one. This has worked time and time again for many of my clients. The answer to that question is to buy investment properties and hold for passive monthly income. I have watched this same strategy create millionaires, and hopefully by following the steps I will give you, it will do the same for you.

How do I buy a property? What type of property should I buy? I want you to know that these steps are given strictly for the beginner, the one who is hungry enough, the one who wants it the most and is ready to make a change in their life, regardless of their current situation. If this is not you, you may be wasting your time reading this book.

To answer the above questions really depends on what you feel most comfortable with, but I do advise all my clients to buy two family homes to start. Two is always better than one and the fact that you can receive two separate rents from under one roof is very beneficial. One of the advantages of buying multi-family properties is that it allows you to have a larger pool of possible tenants due to the fact that the rent rate in multi-family units tend to be a lot lower than a single family home. Another advantage is the cash flow. You will be receiving rent from two tenants or more instead of one and that creates a greater monthly income.

Finally, the most important benefit from owning a multi-family property is that it offers more wiggle room for investors in regards to vacancy. When dealing with a single family home if a tenant moves out you will be liable for all monthly expenses, and if you're at the beginning stages of investing, which I'm sure you are, this is not what you need. I have seen this open and close doors for multiple new investors, but that will not be you.

With a multi-family property, if that same scenario occurs you will still have another tenant in place to help with those expenses, and you will not be 100% liable for all expenses if one tenant decides to move out or does not pay his/her rent. You will not have that benefit from investing in single family homes, regardless of how great the deal may seem.

Now I need to give you a step by step action plan to get you into your first home and future investment property. By this point all the previous steps discussed should have already been taken care of. If not, I advise you to stop right now. Go back to the top and get the ground work done. Look at it this way; can you receive a college degree without ever going to class? I highly doubt it. You would need to do the leg work, which is equivalent to attending and passing all the required courses to become eligible to receive a degree.

Credit is your course and real estate ownership is your degree. Pay attention in class first (credit) and pass, before thinking about moving to the next chapters and receiving a degree (real estate).

Getting Started

There are two ways you can go about getting started. You can be a first time home buyer or a first time investor. Depending on which category you fall, they both require the same strategy, but obtaining financing is alot different.

Let's say you are a first time home buyer. I'm assuming of course, that if you already own a home you would not be reading this book, because you know how important it is to own real estate and how credit is the key to getting there. So, if you are a first time home buyer things just became even easier for you.

To get started you must first understand the benefits that come from being a first time home buyer. One, you qualify for a first time home buyer loan. If you are not sure what that is, allow me to explain. First time home buyer loans offer a low down payment, reduced interest, limited fees and the possibility of deferring payments. These types of loans are offered at a federal level by the Federal Housing Administration (FHA) in most states. One of the key benefits of this loan is that FHA loans are more forgiving of pass mistakes than conventional loans. I have had credit repair clients who receive approval even after filing for bankruptcy in the past.

Another great benefit is that it allows you to keep your monthly cost down. For example, in most cases with an FHA loan mortgage, insurance is funded into the loan, meaning a premium of 1.5% is added on the loan balance instead of being paid out of pocket like most conventional loans.

The greatest benefit is that new borrowers can finance 96.5 percent of the purchase price and put down only 3.5 percent. Now let's say you found a decent duplex that needed small repairs for $120.000. You would only be required to put down 3.5 percent, which would be $4,200, and be on your way to owning your first investment property. I'm sure you know someone right now who has put that same amount down for a rental unit that they would never own or make money from, at least not legally.

Let's Go Get It

This is where you will get your return on your investment from purchasing this book. This section will be your guideline to your first property. I will explain to you in 4 simple steps how to close on your first investment property.

One great thing about the steps you will learn today is that they can be repeated time and time again, resulting in more property's, more cash flow and a better life for you and your family. Mark this section and use it as a reference along the way.

These are the final steps that will change your life from this point on. You have reached the promise land. Grab a pen and paper...don't worry I have time. Ok, you got it? Good. At the top of the paper I want you to write LETS MOVE OR LOSE. This will be your check list. I want you to place this somewhere you visit every day. For me that would be on my refrigerator, but seriously we all know that life can bring unexpected situations which cause us to put dreams and goals on hold. What I have learned about putting things on hold is this; if you have nothing that's constantly reminding you of those things, they will soon be forgotten. This will not happen to you. You will not LOSE. You will MOVE. Take this paper, and as you progress through the rest of the book I want you to number and write out each step that needs to be taken to close on your first investment property. After that, place it somewhere you visit every day. This will act as a constant reminder, and you will begin to dwell on them without even noticing it. The wonderful thoughts of how life could be different if you completed those steps will consume you, and from that you will take action. Always write down your goals and put them where you can see them.

Now, I need you to commit to one more thing. After every completed step, I want you to cross it out and write #WEMADEIT-NEXT. I know it may seem a little corny, but the #WEMADEIT is for you. You did make it. You completed the task. It may have been hard, and you may have questioned if you could do it, but you did. The NEXT is a reminder to never become comfortable, because there's something else that needs to be done.

The Amazing Four Step Guide To Close On Your First Investment Property – After Having All Beginning Steps Completed

STEP 1: Contact A Local Mortgage Company Or Bank And Get Pre- Approved

This is fairly easy to do. I'm sure you pass at least three mortgage company's going to and from work every day. But if not, the easiest way would be to go to www.google.com and type in Mortgage. All mortgage companies within your location will show up with addresses and contact information. Also the FHA official website maintains searchable databases of approved lenders throughout the country. That's another great place to begin your search as well.

After gathering contact information, pick between 3 to 5 lenders who are FHA-approved lenders in your local area. From there start calling them to get the interview process going.

Questions You Should Get The Answers To:

- ✓ How long has the company been active in business?
- ✓ What percentage of loans are FHA loans?
- ✓ What is the experience and time in business of the actually loan officer you speak with?

Request that each lender provide you with a good-faith-estimate, or GFE detailing the quote for your loan. Make sure each lender you contact can provide you with this before choosing. Anyone who refuses, stay away from them.

GFE (is an estimate provided by a lender detailing the anticipated cost associated with any real estate transaction from buying, refinancing or taking out a home equity loan or line of credit).

It's time to get our pens out and slap down the check mark on that to do list with the #WEMADEIT-NEXT.

The first big step is applying to get pre-approved. By this time you should have a clear understanding of all three lenders history and experience. I know you took the time follow each step that was given from the beginning, so I am going to assume you have received your pre-approvals. The next step would be to compare each one. What you will be doing is comparing all good-faith-estimates you received from each lender to see which one works best for you. The way you go about doing this is by simply comparing the quotes on the section labeled "using the shopping cart" that's located on page three of the GFE. This section allows you to compare the annual interest rate and settlement fees for each loan. Each FHA quote will be different. Some may have high interest rates with low settlement fees. Some may have the opposite. So I advise you to weigh the cost and interest rates of the loan with the experience of the loan officer and lender before considering. From there, choose the lender you trust the most with terms that works best for you.

STEP 2: Contact A Local Realtor

This can be done very easy. Start with www.google.com and type Realtors. You will get a list of top realtors in your local market and their company name, addresses and contact information. Next, Google their individual information and find out as much as you possibly can about them before contacting. By doing this, you will know who you are dealing with before speaking with them, which is a good thing. There's no need to waste valuable time. Once that is completed, you should now be able to wing out the potentials from the time wasters before even speaking with them.

Your long list of Google contacts will be cut down drastically. It's time to start making calls and getting familiar with each realtor. I always advise no more than three. That way you can fully focus on the interviewing process, but the final choice is still yours. When going through the interviewing process, remember that this is a person you would be working closely with for the next few months so you want to make sure that the chemistry feels right. If for any reason you feel rushed or a realtor you contacted did not show you much interest, simply remove their name from your list and replace with another. Just about any realtor will be willing to take on your business, including the bad ones due to the fact that you are already pre-approved, so I would advise you not to mention this at the start of the conversation. Doing so could lead to a not so great realtor appearing to be the best. The last thing I would want you to do is make the wrong decision and pay for it later.

Now during the interviewing process, explain to them what you are looking for. Remember, they will be working for you and not the other way around, so make sure you inform exactly what it is you want. Once the conversation has started, and you have a better understanding of who they are, and their history within the business, explain that you're looking to purchase a multi-family property with no more than 4 units. Let them know that this will be your first purchase, and you are looking to occupy one unit. Advise them that you're looking for something with room for equity (which could be a foreclosure with light TLC needed) located in a family community, with steady rental rates. After explaining all that you require, it would be best to find out their history. Ask if they have ever sold properties like this in the past, and if so what was the most recent. You want to make sure that the realtor you choose has experience in this particular field. Now you can inform them that you are already pre-approved for whatever amount the lender has approved you for. From there, the conversation will change, as the hard work from the realtors end is already done so they will consider you as a sure buy. Realtors love clients who are already pre-approved. It makes their job a lot easier because all they have to do now is find the right property and the deal is done. This works out great for you because now all your wants and needs will be attended to a lot quicker than normal. You will be treated as priority #1. But don't forget that you're still new to this game, so you want to remain humble and don't allow the extra attention to change who you are, or your attitude towards the business.

When you complete this step, it's time to make your decision. You should be more familiar with the realtors you interviewed, so choose your realtor and move to Step 3.

Let's get those pins out and slap down the check mark on that to due list with the #WEMADEIT-NEXT.

STEP 3: At This Point You Should Be Receiving Multiple Listings Of Potential Homes From Your Realtor

After reviewing the listings it would be best to pick out a few homes that interest you the most and schedule an appointment to view in person. Remember, a picture tells you nothing. Always review a property in person before you purchase. This will be your first investment property, and you will also be occupying one unit.

There are a few things you must know before considering to purchase.

Location

The quality of the neighborhood in which you purchase will influence both the type of tenants you attract and how often you will face vacancies. It's important that the property you consider to purchase is in a location that has strong rental rates and a demand for rental property. I'm sure you would not want to purchase a property in a location where everyone tends to own a home. What would be your chances of finding renters? Be sure to do your due diligence on the location. It will make or break the success of your property.

Property Taxes

This is also very important and something you want to have the answer to before purchasing. I have watched this time and time again kill a new investor's monthly cash flow because they did not calculate this into effect. You will be looking for a property to make money from by collecting rent monthly, so you want to be aware of how much you will be losing to taxes. Now I don't want you to think that high taxes is always a bad thing because it's not, especially if you're in an excellent location for long term tenants, but you want to make sure you clearly look over this section. Your local assessment office will have tax information on file to help with this process, or you can simply talk to homeowners within the community to get an idea of what they are paying annually.

Schools

It's very likely that your potential tenants will have children, so being located near a great school plays a big part in making sure your unit stays occupied as much as possible. It also works out great for you, if you have a family or plan on starting one soon.

Crime

No one wants to live in a location that's a hot spot for criminal activity. It would be wise to visit the local police station or public library for accurate crime statistics on the property location before considering. Items to look for are vandalism rates, serious crimes, petty crimes, and recent activities. It would also be a good idea to find out if there's police presence in the particular location. Having a property located in a decent area gives your property more value and will attract more renters.

Jobs

Locations with high or growing employment opportunities tend to attract more tenants. Job opportunities means more employees looking to live nearby. Having your property in a location with high employment rates will create an even bigger pool of potential renters for you. To find out how a particular area rates with employment you can visit the U.S. Bureau of Labor Statistics. This will get you on the right tract to obtaining all the information needed about employment within the location.

Rent Rates

Rent will be your bread and butter for a rental property, so knowing the average rent rate is very important when considering a property. If the average rent will not cover your mortgage payment, taxes, and other expenses then the property investment may not be the best idea at all. You will be living in a unit, so there may be a chance that the rent collected monthly will not cover everything because one unit will be occupied by you. You want to make sure that if you were not living there, everything would be covered with no problem.

Those are the six important things to considering before purchasing a property. You should be well on your way to making the best decision on which property will work best for you.

Continue to review all listings that interest you and make sure to take your time while evaluating each and every one them.

We made it! Now go ahead and get those pens out and slap down the check mark on that to do list with the #WEMADEIT-NEXT.

STEP 4: Time to choose!

This by far is the most exciting step of them all. By this point you should have already viewed multiple listings that have interest you. What I would advise you to do now is narrow it down to your top three. A random late night drive by would be a great idea as well if you haven't already done so. It's always a good idea to get familiar with a location during non-working hours. It's normally around those times that you can get a great feel for a neighborhood.

Next, discuss your potential listings with your family or significant other to get their opinion as well. Receiving opinions from friends and family you trust the most is always a great idea, because they can help you see things you didn't see at the beginning. Always remember to make the choice that feels best to you, as this is your investment.

I'm sure you have followed every step needed to make the best decision possible. Now with that said please allow me the opportunity to say congratulations. You made it! I'm sure you're excited. I know I am. Now do me a favor, go ahead and call that realtor and get the closing process started on your new home. #YOUMADEIT!

Final Note

I would like to say thank you for you taking the time to read this book. Some investors may be upset with me because of what I have shared with you, but my only goal is to see you win. I feel one of my purposes on this earth is to help others, and that's what my intensions were for writing this book: To help you succeed and change your financial situation the same way I did.

It's been a long time coming, but I must say you have made it to the end. I'm sure it was not easy, and I'm sure there were times you wanted to give up. You didn't, and that's what I applaud you for the most, your will power.

No matter what life throws at you, I want you to always remember that you can overcome. Real estate is not hard, and it's not only for those who are born rich, and I'm sure you can see that now.

One last thing I ask of you is this: Share the knowledge you have learned from reading this book. Share it with anyone willing to listen. Don't allow the selfish heart to take control. Always remember it's bigger than us. Go into the world, and do great things. Use that credit, use real estate and continue to build.

I will see you at the top.

www.ingramcontent.com/pod-product-compliance
Lightning Source LLC
Chambersburg PA
CBHW070719180526
45167CB00004B/1547